Writing Railways: A short Introduction to Paul Theroux's Travelogues

Writing Railways: A short Introduction to Paul Theroux's Travelogues

Dr. Neema Susan Mathews

NOTION PRESS

India. Singapore. Malaysia.

For my sunshine

Acknowledgment

I raise my hands in praise of the Lord Almighty for guiding me marvellously through the unfamiliar territory and for turning darkness into light. To Him alone be the glory!

I record my boundless and sincere gratitude to my family and all my well-wishers who supported and helped me directly and indirectly to materialise this book.

Contents

Preface

Paul Theroux is a writer whose travelogues are noted for alluring descriptions of intriguing people and vivid landscapes, unexpected encounters and narrow escapes, frequent reflections on the process of writing and more importantly, his passion for rail journeys. Although he is a pioneer of modern travel writing that radically altered the reading public's perception of travelogues, not much studies have been done on his writings. This book is a humble attempt to provide an understanding of the cultural aspects of railways, of Paul Theroux as a travel writer and his select texts.

1
Railways and Culture

The railroad is that work of an art which agitates and drives mad the whole people; as music, sculpture and picture have done on their great days respectively.

Ralph Waldo Emerson, "Journal LM"

Since the early nineteenth century, railways have been is one of the major transport systems that facilitated both transnational and national movements, criss-crossing the nooks and crannies, into the heart of the people by "abolishing time, distance and delay" (Smith 349). Railway's significant presence can be found in numerous poems, fiction, non-fiction, paintings, photographs and films. The focus of study on the American travel writer Paul Theroux's rail journeys, calls for an exploration of the emblematic presence of railroads in world culture, mainly the American. This chapter intends to present a brief outline of the multifarious representations of this particular technology of movement in literature.

Ever since its introduction in America, railways permeate the vast spectrum of artistic, social and cultural practices. Though ingrained in the routines of daily life, at times, technology becomes a subject of human consciousness and imaginations. While some artisans celebrated the new tempo of modernity, some lamented over it as the end of the art of travel. The painters from the nineteenth century tried to imagine railroads being integrated into the American pastoral scenery, while the writers expressed their ambivalence toward the rail-technology in their works. In literature, trains function not just as a mode of transport like cars or buses but as a symbol with many implications. Trains add a deeper layer to the narrative surface, as that is where people usually accidentally meet, separate their ways, take time to ponder, work on something, and find a place of rest and relaxation.

From a survey conducted on the literary responses towards railways since its introduction in the American soil, Ian Marshall observes that there is a cycle of response ranging from "decry[ing] railroads as despoilers of the vast landscapes", celebrat[ing] as a means of extending the national domain and preserving national unity", "link[ing] manufacturing centers to agrarian districts", criticising the "alienation brought by the profits of technology" and finally, in the second half of the 20th century, "regard[ing] it as a thing of the past" (38), an object evoking nostalgia. Marshall beholds that

America's literature about railroads takes on the structure of a wheel, revolving from concern to appreciation to condemnation to appreciation again. . . [They] have consistently seemed to be of two minds about railroads, or, to phrase it another way, their thinking has followed parallel tracks of praise and blame (ibid).

Emerson retains a positive attitude towards railways, applauding the power, energy, wonder and enthusiasm they impart. "Railroad iron is a magician's rod in its power to evoke the sleeping energies of land and water" ("The Young American" 364), he notes. He also records the irreplaceable role of railways in holding the vast North America together during the Mexican war. Unlike in England, where railroads followed the already established roads, in America, it was constructed through country lands as they were being developed.

The Americans' association with railways was more intimate than the Europeans, as it linked the country people to the mainstream. Within a relatively short span of time, rail transportation altered the way Americans lived, taking them closer to far off goods, closer to each other, and impelled them to accept a uniform system of time zones. The democratic nature of American railways is evident in its architecture too.

American trains contained a microcosm of society in contrast to the class - segregated, compartmentalised passengers. Emerson celebrated the spirit of democracy that American railways propagated and reflected on how nature eventually accommodates technology. Interestingly, he also acknowledges the loss of freedom that railways impose on passengers by keeping them on fixed paths.

Thoreau, the artist of the wild who is usually critical of materialistic values, upholds railways for its "regularity and precision", "punctuality" and describes it as a well conducted institution which regulates a whole country (*On Walden Pond* 138). Nevertheless, like Emerson, he also talks about the threats that railways produce by distorting country land. In *The House of Seven Gables* (1851), Nathaniel Hawthorne enunciates his concerns through two characters - Hepzibah and Pyncheon who ride a train. Hawthorne shares his conflicting thoughts with Thoreau and Emerson. Emily Dickinson's poem "I like to see it lap the miles" (1862) and Walt Whitman's poem, "To a Locomotive in Winter" (1876) showcase railways in ambiguous ways.

In the first half of the twentieth century, railways appear less in the literature, if at all it was written, the trend continued to be the same as the previous century. In 1906, the "Railroad Man's Magazine" was published, featuring 'true-to-life' stories about daily routines, vexations and adventures, along with a few non-fiction explicating the meaning of signals, the braking systems and fuelling. By 1937, the "Railroad Man's Magazine" became "Railroad Magazine" and it attracted a wider audience. Stilgoe observes that "Americans, especially boys and men, found in the literature a gateway into the seemingly romantic life of the railroad right-of-way" (5). Edward Channing's *Elements of United States of History*, a 1919 textbook for school children affirms the significance of railroads in developing the nation. The struggle of a boy caught up in between the agrarian world of his father, and the romantic world of railways is well captured in Harold Waldo's autobiography, *The Magic Midland* (1923). This ignored novel also reflects the nation's transition from the rural to the industrial age.

The toy electric trains by the Lionel Corporation played a major role in bringing the essence of the railroad to every other home. Founded in 1900, the firm made even more realistic and sophisticated models of the American steam and electric locomotives, passenger cars and freight trains. Stilgoe notes that at least several hundred thousand families erected permanent layouts of model tracks in their cellars or attics during that time (12).

While the above-mentioned American writers ruminated on a set of themes around the progress that the railways brought into the American soil, the African-American writers have a different story to tell. "Runagate Runagate", a haunting poem written by Robert Hayden, an African-American writer, portrays the underground railroad, portrays the underground railroad that was used in the middle 1800s to aid the slaves in escaping to the north to freedom via a secret network. It depicts the African-Americans' social, political, legal, psychological and spiritual struggle against white supremacy. The narrator of the poem, Harriet Tubman, a woman, calls forth her children to ride the train, which is portrayed as a vehicle that can lead them to ultimate freedom. "Of the Coming of John" is a

1903 story written by W. E. B. Du Bois in the background of railways. The story ends with a sad scene of the protagonist, John, an African-American slave walking towards the sea to escape from his sad plight. In this story, the train becomes a symbol of a broken promise and lies. Darcy Zabel observes:

> twentieth-century African-American writers have self-consciously chosen to use the train as a symbol because of the importance of the train in American history, the popular and scholarly interest in the Underground railroad, the need for legendary black heroes and heroines that can be met by an examination of train folklore, and the metaphoric possibilities associated with trains, tracks and the modern underground. (6)

Thus, we see how the symbol of the train is treated in literature across ages and races. This can be further explained with Wolfgang Iser's concept of literary symbols.

In *The Fictive and the Imaginary*, Iser shows how a symbol contains "inherited schemata" that "reproduce[s] affective attitudes, memories, knowledge, mental and perceptual dispositions" (254). Members of a particular discourse community "inherit" symbols with its meanings and use it in their communication. American politicians and railroad companies always advertised train as an icon of advancement and the same idea is varyingly echoed in the writings of the white writers like Thoreau, Emerson, and Whitman.

Leo Marx, in one of his essays elucidates how the press and popular writers helped to keep up their enthusiasm for railways, propagating an "ideological purpose", hushing the reports of "far reaching economic and social consequences" (184). But African-American writers choose not to carry over the set of meanings that already exists in the white world, and they create their own meanings for a symbol, adding layers of signification. When the new meanings are repeated in literature, they also become a part of the "inherited schemata" of that particular community.

After the world wars and dismissal of colonies, railways reappeared in prints with a tint of nostalgia. Sinclair Lewis in *Main Street* (1920) writes during the apogee of the railroads: "It was hurling past-the Pacific Flyer, an arrow of golden flame. Light from the fire-box splashed the underside of the trailing smoke. Instantly the vision was gone" (236). Carl Sandburg expresses his optimism in his poems, such as "Caboose Thoughts" and "Work Gangs". These railroad poems celebrate the lives of the workers who tirelessly toil to build America. In the poem "Child of the Romans", he presents an ironical situation by contrasting the image of a shovel man eating dry bread and bologna with a scene from a dining car, "steaks running with brown gravy, / Strawberries and cream, éclairs and coffee" (12). The juxtaposition of the rich and the poor refers to the dichotomous reality of the society. Archibald MacLeish's "Grazing Locomotives", Hart Crane's "The Bridge", Joyce Kilmer's "The Twelve-Forty-Five" and Ogden Nash's "Riding on a railroad train" are some of the notable poems that come later with the same theme.

When railroads were replaced by other forms of transport by 1930, the values that were assigned to the functions of the railway such as 'building nation' was also displaced. Stilgoe points out an example through the changes that occurred in the usages in the language:

> In 1900, nearly everyone called the intersection of a railroad and road a *road crossing*; the term connotes the dominant perception of space seen from a train. By 1910, the term *grade crossing* had replaced the earlier one, except in the speech of railroad employees and in the pages of popular railroad fiction. Within two decades, however, *railroad crossing* had almost totally replaced both the earlier terms, announcing the newly dominant perception of space seen from the motor car. . . . A great age of automobile-shaped spatial design dawned, and the era of the corridor ended. . . . a once-great environment, abandoned to wilderness, decayed almost unmourned. (339)

In England, the case was not different. The country witnessed a rapid development of railway construction between 1840 and 1860, the period known as 'the railway age'. The Victorians associated the railways with progress and civilisation. Charles Dickens presents a pessimistic, imaginative view of railway travel in *Dombey and Sons* (1848). He saw it as a ubiquitous but devouring technology that ruins the idyllic nature of England.

With the arrival of railways, new perspectives of time and space were derived. As the train connected hitherto faraway places within a short period of time, it created anxiety in the passengers with regard to speed and pace. The society saw the train as an assemblage of dichotomies of progress and degeneration, engendering fear and excitement in people. The perplexing attitude towards train was evident in contemporary literature. Though he did not write anything on the topic of train, Robert Browning is known to be a fervent rail traveller. Matthew Arnold was not in favour of this technological phenomenon as he saw it as an icon of the philistine nature of the age. An element of dissolution was seen in George Eliot's *Middlemarch* (1871-72) and Thomas Hardy's novels too. In Jules Verne's *Around the World in Eighty Days* (1873), Phineas Fogg begins and ends his journey on trains, and also depends on them to carry him across India (from Bombay to Calcutta), and the US (from San Francisco to New York). Leo Tolstoy's *Anna Karenina* (1877) has a crucial episode at a station. Agatha Christie makes Poirot solve a particularly difficult case in the train in *Murder on the Orient Express* (1934). Recently, a literary train journey has become very popular through the Harry Potter series. The Hogwarts Express, the train that makes a run between London, King's Cross Station Platform 9¾ and Hogsmeade Station dutifully carries students to and from the Hogwarts School of Witchcraft and Wizardry at the start and end of every term. The depiction of the vintage train refreshes the fading image of railways in readers' minds.

When it comes to India, though a by-product and a souvenir of British rule, the railway has completely become an Indian cultural icon in every sense as Arup K Chatterji writes in his book *Purveyors of Destiny*: "[w]hat imperialism made opulent, nationalism embraced as a swadeshi tool, partition turned into theatres of macabre, and the nation's destiny marked for its favourite foster child, came to embody the portable architecture of India's modernity". The railways represented a Western, non-traditional and destructive entity, especially for Mahatma Gandhi. In *Hind Swaraj and Other Writings* (1909), he vehemently denounces railways. But the irony is that it is the railways that connect him to the entire country of India and enables his visit to the remote villages, thereby sharing his message to millions of people. And eventually, he modifies his attitude, "(w)hat I object to, is the craze for machinery, not machinery as such" (170). Richard Cronin in *Imagining India* (1989) comments on the role of railways in nation-building: "Dalhousie planned the railways to tighten British rule of India, to make it more efficient. But the trains had one effect that Dalhousie surely did not foresee. They made possible the birth of the idea that was finally to put an end to the Raj, the idea that India was a nation" (77). Paul Theroux supports the fact that railways hold a binding power in the nation - "India works because the railway works" (*GTES* 158). He considers railways as a comparatively dependable mode of transportation in India.

Tainted with local flavour, the railway undergoes the process of transculturation and continual negotiation across the countries. Ian Carter states that "(b)orn in Britain, the modern railway's machine ensemble bundled together many different technical, economic and social novelties in that place. But the modern railway picked up subtly different inflections as export trades developed, coloured by local meanings in other national jurisdictions" (12). This becomes evident in the cultural expressions such as literature and movies of the particular society, especially in India.

The colonial writers like Rudyard Kipling and Flora Annie Steel, nationalists Rabindranath Tagore and Mohandas Gandhi, post-Independence writers like R. K Narayan, Anita Nair and Jhumpa Lahiri employ the railway in their writings. In *Kim* (1901), the main characters Kim and the Lama, as well as some other characters, travel by train throughout the country, thereby providing a vivid picture of railways and the state of British India. The English travel writers during the colonial times have recorded the Indian way of utilizing the public space of the railway. In their point of view, Aguiar notes, "Indians mobbed the stations, talked excessively, brought their pots and pans, and turned the secular world of the train into a place for religious rituals" (30).

John W Mitchell in 1934 writes:

> [w]e sip our tea, looking through the carriage windows to watch the Indian passengers dashing hither and thither in that aimless way which seems to obsess them, at all time, on a railway station platform when the train is in.
>
> Pandemonium reigns.

> A bedlam of sound fills the morning air. There, an excited Hindu calls to his household, who run trembling after him with their pots, pans and other chattels hanging around them, like so many iterant gypsy vendors. (21-22)

Mitchell's description of the Indian railway scenes is analogous to Theroux's narratives on the unrestrained disorder and chaos of the same. The antagonism towards the Indian passengers is a colonial trope which is present in the rail narratives since Empire. At the same time, Bholonauth Chunder, an Indian writer in *Travels of a Hindoo to various parts of Bengal and Upper India* (1869) captures the reception of the railway:

> Travelling by the rail very much resembles migrating in one vast colony, or setting out together in a whole moving town or caravan. Nothing under this enormous load is ever tagged to the back of a locomotive, and yet we were no sooner in motion than Calcutta, and the Hooghly, and Howrah, all began to recede away like the scenes in a Dissolving View. . . . the Hindoo look upon the railways as a marvel and miracle -a novel incarnation for the regeneration of *Bharat-versh* (qtd. in Manu Goswami 103).

The railways play a vital role during India-Pakistan partition as many refugees flee to the two countries in packed trains. Khushwant Singh's *Train to Pakistan* (1956) and Mukul Kesavan's *Looking Through Glass* (1995) painfully reflect the bleeding reality from the partition period. The railway becomes a carrier of violence in these works. It attains a horrific semblance, entirely different from its original conception as a bearer of modernity and secularism. Rohinton Mistry's *A fine balance* (1995) is about the political unrest during 1975-1985 and the railway helping in transporting and uniting people. The Indian novels set on trains are few and far in between compared to those in other nations. The railways are yet to receive the attention they deserve from the Indian authors.

The innovations in technologies of travel are certain factors that have been dominant in the shaping of travel writing since 1900. "This in turn resulted in a narrative self-consciousness about how they travelled previously and now. Not infrequently, texts go beyond comment on the means of travel and reflect on the appropriateness of the literary vehicle itself" (Youngs, *Cambridge Introduction* 69). As railways developed and made connections across nations, there was a tremendous growth in books dealing with the particularities of railways. There emerged writers who focussed more on the technological aspect of the train than the social experience. George Behrend (*Railway Holiday in France*, 1964), Bryan Morgan (*The End of the Line: A Book About railways and Places Mainly Continental*, London: Cleaver-Hulme, 1955) and Norman McKillop (*Western Rail Trail*, 1962) wrote on the working of the machine and the workers of railways.

In the second half of the twentieth century, when flying across places became more common and popular, a few travel writers chose to seek places and cultures using trains, thus making train an aesthetic choice. Paul

Theroux pioneers them with his first book, *The Great Travel Bazaar* which was published in 1975. He stands apart from other travel writers - "(m)ine was to be the ultimate book about getting there" (*OPE* viii). He shows more interest in recording the onward journey than narrating the destination. Hence, he "sought trains" and "found passengers" (*GRB* 12). Many writers followed him such as George F Scheer (*Booked on the Morning train: A Journey through America*, 1991), Mary Morris (*Wall to Wall: From Beijing to Berlin by rail*, 1992), Miles Bredin (*Blood on the Tracks: A rail Journey from Angola to Mozambique*, 1994), Henry Kisor (*Zephyr: Tracking a Dream across America*, 1994), Richard Nye, (*Rail blazing*, 1994), Terry Pindell, and Lourdes Ramires Mallis (*Yesterday's train: A rail Odyssey through Mexican History*, 1997). There are writers like Thomas Murphy who favour automobile travel over journeying by rail. Murphy in his *British Highways and Byways from a Motor Car* (1909) chooses automobile over the railways as it grants him a closer view of nature than that provided by trains.

In the study of travel writings, the spaces and technologies that facilitate movement usually go unnoticed. Often their main focus is more on the observations made by the traveller than on the background elements like the infrastructure that enables the journeys. The mode of travel that is, "the spaces and technologies that facilitate travel" (Vandertop 129) has not been a topic of study in travel narratives until recently. Infrastructure can be defined "[a]s the driving circulatory and connective forces of modernity. . ..[it] operate[s] as complex assemblages, channelling flows of energy, goods, people and information across shrinking distances" (Vandertop 130).

The infringement of infrastructure, as in the case of Paul Theroux, the railways, calls for critical attention for Forsdick observes:

> The chosen mode of transport continues to have implications not only for the experience of the journey but also for the poetics of the travel narrative. The proliferation of means of transport may, for instance, permit a variegation of the travelogue, as the narrator's perception of and engagement with the field of travel alters according to his or her relative velocity or sense of removal from or proximity to the surroundings. (71)

One of the factors that have been dominant in the shaping of travel writing since 1900 is the innovation in the technologies for travel. Often the mode of transport becomes an instrumental element in the formation of a travel narrative. "… [T]he type of transport taken influences how people travel and how they write up their travels. Journeys by foot, horseback, ship, stagecoach, train…each result in accounts that owe something of their structure and perspective to the mode and pace of motion" (Youngs, *Cambridge Introduction* 171). By the turn of the twentieth century, the motor cars and aeroplanes replaced the old mode of transport like travelling by foot, horseback, steamship, railway, which prompted Jonathan Raban to say- "It's easy to talk blithely about casting oneself adrift in the world; not quite so easy to do it in practice, when most methods of transport turn the would-be traveller into a human bullet" (227). However, some writers consciously challenge the new trends in transportation modes by returning to the older forms of travel. While writers like Bruce Chatwin, Paul Theroux, Philip Glazebrook and Eric Newby use railways, Dervla Murphy tours the countries with a bicycle and Raban in a sailing vessel.

D. H Lawrence in *Sea and Sardinia* gets excited on a ship, to face the vast and boundless sea, far away from a "life among tense, resistant people on land". Lawrence becomes expressionistic and impulsive as his "heart beats with joy" when he feels the "slow lift of the ship" and the "slow slide forwards" (*Sea and Sardinia* 30). Lawrence's liberating experience can be contrasted with Theroux's journeys on the eastbound trains. Theroux is occupied with the impressions of the physical and mechanical world - " . . . the sound of a train at night, striking the precise musical note of train whistles, a diminished third, into the darkness, as you lie in the train, moving through the world as travellers do, 'inside the whale" (*GTES* 3). Lawrence and Theroux use different modes of transport, and it is reflected in their respective narratives. The contributing presence of infrastructure, - the railways, offers critical possibilities for reading Theroux.

Wolfgang Schivelbusch, the German scholar in his highly original and engaging book, *The Railway Journey* (1977) examines the origins of the industrialised consciousness by exploring the public response in the nineteenth century to the first dramatic incarnation of technological change, the railroad. Grounded in European traditions of critical sociology, Schivelbusch studies the ways in which our perceptions of distance, time, speed, autonomy, and risk are amended by railway travel. As an account of the astounding ways in which technology and culture interact, this book covers a wide range of topics, including the changing perception of landscapes, the death of conversation while travelling, the problematic nature of the railway compartment, the space of glass architecture, the pathology of the railway journey, industrial fatigue and the history of shock, and the railroad and the city. The study aims to understand the learned behaviour of the industrial society in the context of railways.

John Stilgoe, through his book *Metropolitan Corridor* (1983) studies the American built environment being constructed along the American railways over the fifty years after 1880. "Trains", Stilgoe notes, "right-of-way and adjacent built form had become part environment, part experience, a combination perhaps best called metropolitan (ix). In addition to the pre-existing division of environment into rural, suburban and urban, trains and right-of-way creates a "fourth distinctive environment- the metropolitan corridor" (x). Reaching from the centre of great cities across industrial zones, suburbs, small towns, coastal areas and into mountain wilderness and nothingness, the metropolitan corridor developed around railways imparts a new lifestyle to the land.

The Railway Station: A Social history (1986) written by Jeffrey Richards and John MacKenzie focuses on stations as generators of new value in the society. They present a social history of railway stations by treating them "not as inanimate objects, but as living, breathing places" (vi), following the advice of Rudyard Kipling: "Make the platform speak. It should have some tales to tell" (qtd. in Richards and Mackenzie viii). Railway stations have not got their due recognition for their contribution to both railway systems in particular and culture and society in general. Many railway stations like Chhatrapati Shivaji Maharaj Terminus in Mumbai, that are mostly uilt-in revival styles- Gothic, Classical, Renaissance, Baroque, exemplify the nineteenth century's distinctive contribution to architectural forms. Mostly stations reflect the societies around them. In the twentieth century, the previous architectural styles and forms disappeared to follow the dictum of 'functionalism' where stations were erected using plastic, concrete etc. In the West, the majestic stations have become endangered. Yet the third world, especially Thailand, Malaya and even India take efforts to preserve their monumental stations. The motorcar which replaced trains inspired no great architecture and no great art which where a railway station's significance is affirmed.

Michael Freeman and Ian Carter in their works, *Railways and the Victorian Imagination* (1999) and *Railways and Culture in Britain* (2001) respectively, explore the cultural implications of railways in the context of modernity. Freeman's aim is "to re-engage the railway with the age of which it was a part,"(19) and he uses "the experience of the railway" and "the railway as cultural metaphor" (25), as a means of executing that end. The book begins with an appraisal of the railway as a challenge to the status quo, both social and natural. In *Railways and culture in Britain*, Ian Carter looks into the cultural impact of train technology, and how this was represented in British society. His survey across obvious and obscure literary and artistic references to trains and railways suggests the profundity of influence railroads had on human consciousness. "By triangulating railway historians' work with material from literary critics, art historians and social theorists", Carter intends to "lay out a less cramped agenda for railway studies: an agenda which takes culture more seriously than in most previous work" (7).

Many journals solely committed to transport studies such as *The Journal of Transport History* published by the Manchester University Press reveal the growing sensitivity towards railways in the academic and cultural realm. *The Journal of Transport History* aims to expand the understanding of agency and impacts in transport history by documenting and explaining moments, phases, trends and pivots in it. In 2007, Matthew Beaumont and Michael Freeman published *The Railway and Modernity: Time, Space, and the Machine Ensemble*. The authors in the collection aim to explore the railways as a key signifier of capitalist modernity. They attempt to study social relations where the railway is historically embedded, recognising it as the main problem in the cultural experience of modernity.

When the railways were introduced in the nineteenth century, it fashioned a change in the field of vision and its representation in aesthetics. It opened a new world of optical entertainment. It took a while for the human sensorium to get adapted to the speed of onrushing moving images. The transformed vision caused by this rapid transport system led to a series of discussions, analysing the quality and intensity of the visual experience.

The advent of the railroad had a pervasive impact on human culture in the Western and Eastern hemisphere as it tremendously affected the experiences of space and time, economic production, the course of historical events, and the contours of social propinquity.

Railway as a technology that brought revolutionary changes in the world has been studied historically, socially and economically but not much has been done on contextualizing the railways in terms of cultural studies. The train is not merely an icon of industrial progress or a metaphor/symbol for the opposing values of modernity but also a subject worthy of cultural analysis.

2

Theroux and Texts

The son of a French-Canadian father, Albert Eugene, a shoe-leather salesman and an Italian mother, Anne Dittami, a former school teacher, Paul Edward Theroux was born on April 10, 1941, in Medford, Massachusetts. His family was not only populous but talented and motivated. Theroux's own branch of family produced several writers - Paul, his novelist older brother Alexander, and his younger brother Peter, a travel writer – as well as another brother who became a businessman in China. Theroux remembers a childhood of freedom but with little privacy. The overprotection of his family used to suffocate him. In *Fresh Air Fiend* he writes :

Raised in a large, talkative, teasing family of seven children, I yearned for space of my own. One of my pleasures was reading; reading was a refuge and an indulgence. But my greatest pleasure lay in leaving my crowded house and going for all-day hikes. In time these hikes turned into camping trips. Fortunately our house was at the edge of town, so I could go out the front door and after half a mile of walking be in the woods, attractively named the Mystic Fells. On my own, I had a clearer sense of who I was, and I had a serious curiosity about what I found in the woods. (1-2)

After graduating from high school, Theroux attended the University of Massachusetts where he became involved in the nascent anti-war movement. He was arrested for leading a student anti-war demonstration. Graduating from college in 1963, he taught in Italy for a short time. Afterwards, he joined the Peace Corps and was sent to Limbe, Malawi, in South Central Africa where he taught English. It was in Africa, as a young volunteer in this unknown country, that he embarked on his writing career. He wrote articles for African papers as well as the Christian Science Monitor and created his own English teaching text.

When I went to Africa, a young man and unpublished, I became a mzungu, or white man, but the Chichewa word also implies a spirit, a ghost figure, almost a goblin, a being so marginal as to be barely human. I did not find it at all hard to accept this definition; I had always felt fairly marginal, with something to prove. So, speaking about myself as a traveller is the most logical way of speaking about myself as a writer. (Ibid 2)

In 1965, his polemical writings caused some political issues and he was deported from Malawi and also faced expulsion from the Peace Corps. It was in Uganda where he met his wife, Anne, a fellow teacher and a broadcaster. They got married in 1967, the same year his first novel, Waldo, was published. In the debut novel, a significant theme that runs pervasive in many of Theroux's works is established: the attempt of man to put some order and meaning to his life. Waldo was followed by the second novel in 1968, Fong and the Indians, set in Kenya. It is the story of Sam Fong, a Chinese Catholic living in Africa, revolved around his plight as an expatriate. Girls at Play, Theroux's next novel is a tragedy, about the story of five white schoolteachers who reached Kenya to teach at a school for African girls. A crucial fact about Theroux's African life is that it was in Uganda where he met the writer V. S. Naipaul, who became his mentor and friend for the next thirty years. Soon, Theroux had to leave Africa as a protest has initiated against the whites. He then moved on to Asia.

It was during his twenties that Theroux became obsessed with the idea of travel - "The idea of disappearance appealed to me. For about ten years, the whole decade of my twenties, I was utterly out of touch. I went to central Africa in 1963 and stayed for five years, and then instead of heading home I went to Singapore" (*Ibid* 3). While he taught English at the University of Singapore, he published a novel with an African title, Jungle Lovers (1971). Theroux's preoccupation with the settings and theme of Conrad's novels is evident in Jungle Lovers. In 1971, having published five novels, Theroux decided to quit teaching and move to Singapore. After living in Singapore for a few years, he left for England where he indulged in writing novels, essays, and book reviews. Then he published a Singapore novel, Saint Jack with the narrator and principal protagonist, Jack Flowers as an exile. About his secluded London life, he writes:

> During this entire period, living frugally, I did not own a telephone, and the few calls I made were all in the nature of emergencies - reporting births and deaths, summoning doctors, all on borrowed phones. This decade of being off the phone, which is the most extreme condition of being cut off, was formative for

me, one of the best things that could have happened in my passage to becoming a writer, because it forced on me a narrow sort of life from which there was no turning back. I was isolated and enlightened. I learned to cope, I read more, I wrote more, I had no TV, I thought in a more concentrated way, I lived in one place, and I studied patience. (Ibid 3-4)

During the ten years in London, Theroux underwent a metamorphosis. He prepared for a long solo journey, disconnected from the rest of the world, including his own family. In 1973, he embarked on a grand tour by train - a journey from London to Tokyo and back which marks the beginning of his endless expedition. Based on his travel, he published *The Great Railway Bazaar* in 1975. He has since written a number of other travel books, including descriptions of travelling by train from Boston to Argentina -*The Old Patagonian Express* (1979), walking around the United Kingdom - *The Kingdom By The Sea* (1983), kayaking in the South Pacific - *The Happy Isles Of Oceania* (1992), visiting China - *Riding the Iron Rooster* (1988) and *Sailing Through China* (1984), travelling from Cairo to Cape Town - *Dark Star Safari* (2013) and *Last Train to Zona Verdana* (2013) and retracing his first travel route - *Ghost Train to the Eastern Star* (2009). When Theroux published his first travel text, GRB in 1975, it marked a new trend in the genre. To introduce a new form for the book, he decided "on a series of train journeys" (GRB X) that feature "lots of people and dialogue and no sightseeing" (GRB vii-viii). Since then he has written many travel books in the same form including *The Old Patagonian Express, Dark Star Safari, Ghost Train to the Eastern Star* and *The Last Train to Zona Verde.*

Meanwhile, Theroux had published numerous works of fiction, some of which were later made into feature films. One of Theroux's most popular novels is *The Mosquito Coast* (1981).It is a story told from the point of view of the thirteen-year-old son of an American, Allie Fox. Fox takes his family into exile from modernity to the jungles of Honduras. The novel was made into a movie starring Harrison Ford. *The Mosquito Coast* established Theroux's name as a novelist with the general public, especially the American public just as *The Great Railway Bazaar* did for him as a travel writer.

O-zone, a novel published in 1986, is science fiction. In 1989, Theroux published the first of his autobiographies, *My Secret History,* followed the next year by *Chicago Loop,* a story of a serial killer who ultimately turns against himself. Divorced in 1993, Theroux returned to live in the United States after living abroad for nearly thirty years. In 1994, he published *Millroy the Magician,* another book told from a youthful perspective. His subsequent works of fiction are *Kowloon Tong* (1997), a political thriller involving twoBritish expatriates living in Hong Kong, *Hotel Honolulu* (2001) which revolves around a middle-aged writer from the mainland who leaves behind his family and old life to start over in Hawaii, *Sir Vidia's Shadow: A Friendship across Five Continents* (1998), in which Theroux portrays his association with V. S. Naipaul (Sir Vidia), the author's one-time mentor and friend of more than thirty years. In 2000, Theroux published a collection of travel essays under the title *Fresh Air Fiend: travel writings, 1985-2000*; the work covered the author's adventures on five continents and over the waters in between. In 2001, Theroux came up with a very different work of nonfiction in *Nurse Wolf and Dr. Sacks. The Elephant Suite (2007)* is a novel based in India. In

Mother Land (2017) he portrays a family held together and torn apart by its narcissistic matriarch.

The critic, Paul Fussel, in his study of travel writers who wrote between the World Wars, observes that many of them - D H Lawrence, Evelyn Waugh, and Robert Byron despise the technological impact on the society for they have witnessed how technology brought atrocities during world wars. They yearned for the world outside civilization. Fussel also argues that post-1945, "real' travel was no more possible, thus also implicating the end of the travel writing industry too. However, proving his prediction wrong, travel writing flourished tremendously towards the end of the twentieth century. Majority of them bring back the images of otherness once popularised by the colonial writers.

Travelogues provide some writers "sanctuary from contemporary 'politically correct' attitudes about race, gender, sexuality and class" (Lisle, *Global* 19). Theroux uses travel writing as a vehicle to take him to foreign places where he then travels back in time. The superficial cosmopolitanism of Theroux's travel narratives is arrested by a historical mode which is essentially regressive.

Theroux is known to be responsible for the revitalisation of the popularity of travel writing in the late twentieth century (Youngs, *The Cambridge Introduction* 79). He identifies the Western society's need for alternatives to fight the "growing fears of homogenization" and proficiently introduces a new form of travel writing, that gives validity for the notion that the world is still "heterogeneous, unfathomable [and] bewildering" (Holland and Huggan 2). He chooses an appropriate mode of travel, trains to travel around the world. When Theroux published his first travel text, *The*

Great Railway Bazaar in 1975, it marked a new trend in the genre. He decides "on a series of train journeys" (*GRB* x) that features "lots of people and dialogue and no sightseeing" (vii-viii). The passage of a subjective body in a mass transportation system – railways, is the basic scheme of Theroux's narratives.

Theroux attempts to convince the readers that he is trying to do something different from other travel writers. He says, "Feeling cheated that way by other travel books, and wondering what exactly it is I have been denied, I decided to experiment by making my way to travel-book country, as far south as the trains run from Medford, Massachusetts; to end my book where travel books begin" (*OPE* 14).

In the first chapter of *OPE,* Theroux mentions three books - *The Man-Eaters of Tsavo* by Lt Col J.H. Patterson, *Duty Preserved* by Mollie Panter-Downes and *Which Tribe Do You Belong To* by Alberto Moravia in which he is unable to find the descriptions of 'the going'- that is the journey from home towards destinations. He makes a critical note, "[t]he literature of travel has become measly, the standard opening that farcical nose-against-the-porthole view from the plane's tilted fuselage. The joke-opening, that straining for effect, is now so familiar it is nearly impossible to parody" (*OPE* 12).

By challenging the existing pattern of travel writing, Theroux creates a new form of travelogue, of 'going', not arriving - "mine was to be the ultimate book about getting there" (*OPE* VIII). More than the destination, Theroux's narrative is devoted to the poetics of motion. If so, the mode of travel matters much in the narratives.

In *The Great Indian Bazaar,* Theroux embarks on a four-month trip from London, through Europe and into Turkey, to Iran, Pakistan and India. He travels extensively in India and then flies to Rangoon, Burma. There, he sees the Gokteik Viaduct and then flies to Thailand, and takes rails all the way to Singapore. He makes a halt in Vietnam and travels on some parts of the Trans-Vietnam railway. He travels expansively in Japan and after a sea voyage, takes the long Trans-Siberian railroad back to Europe and London.

From the beginning of the book, the author expresses great delight in riding railroad trains - "(t)rains seemed the happiest choice" (vii). To stand apart from the contemporary travel writings, Theroux "envision[s] a long book with lots of people and dialogue and no sightseeing" (*GRB* vii). On the train, he meets passengers, both natives and tourists. He enjoys observing the scenery from the train through the windows. The railways in the Western and Eastern Europe have inferior service, since this means of travel is now considered almost obsolete. The train stations in Bulgaria and Yugoslavia are made interesting by the people there and the food that is offered for sale. Other stations are imposing landmarks by themselves. He remarks that in India, villages literally exist in railway stations. Reflecting on the religious status, the station in Kuala Lumpur, Malaysia is built in the form of a huge mosque. The train travel is excellent in Turkey and Iran. In Pakistan and Iran, many women are veiled and men engage in a weird habit of staring at women on the billboards and in the strip clubs. As the author's travel progresses, the challenges and difficulties faced by him keep increasing. Theroux finds himself on an uncertain quest when he seeks to cross the Gokteik Viaduct in Northern Burma. The tunnels and topography of the Khyber Pass railroad and the vastness of the Trans-Siberian railroad give the narrative a beautiful lustre.

The characters whose names have to be mentioned are Mr. Molesworth and the unfortunate Mr Duffill, who misses getting back on the train in Italy after purchasing lunch bags from the platform. The temporality of meetings with co-passengers imparts exclusivity to the companionship that Theroux develops. The consumption of liquor and food opens new avenues for Theroux to indulge in conversations. It takes him four months to travel, note down his impressions and later a year to write the book. In the course of his travels, he makes stops in many cities where he delivers lectures on American literature which provides him with monetary benefits to supplement his travels. His steady co-operation with the local U.S. Embassies and Consulates ensures a trouble-free and seamless travel. The overall mood of the travelogue is that of exploration and adventure, which gives the impression that the whole trip is risky and unusual.

With one 'travel-by-train' book successfully completed, Theroux decides to embark on writing another one, this time, to "remain in the Western Hemisphere" and "make a connection between known and the unknown" (*OPE* vi). His second travel book, *The Old Patagonian Express* (*OPE*) was published in 1979. *OPE* starts from Medford, Massachusetts, where he catches the train at Wellington Circle just after a blizzard has dumped snow in the area. On the subway train, in which the daily commuters are on their way to work or shop, Theroux begins his adventure trip to Patagonia. Similar to his first text, he utilizes the first few pages of OPE to contemplate on the generic characteristics of a travel book and the purpose it serves for the writer and the reader. The narrative gains momentum as time passes. Theroux thinks that by travelling on a train, he can hold a grip over the passing space and time, as opposed to a plane trip which transports passengers in a concealed state. Besides the sights that are seen through the train's window, he describes the people riding with him. As the Amtrak express runs late, he is offered a stay at the Holiday Inn (an expensive hotel). He appears to be restless being stuck in wintry Chicago. It convinces him that "the sooner … [he] got to the savage jungle, however dark and bitter, the better" (*OPE* 35). He is not happy with his cosy stay in Chicago and wants to go South soon.

From Chicago, the train makes a turn for the south through mid-America. Winter's pressure is apparent throughout the passing landscape. The Amtrak line ends at Laredo, a town which appears to be more Mexican than Texan. At the very moment he steps on the frontier, the border between Mexico and the USA, a sense of estrangement catches him, for he says:

Looking south, across the river, I realised that I was looking towards another continent, another country, another world. There were sounds there - music, and not only music but the pip and honk of voices and cars. The frontier was actual: people did things differently there, and looking hard I could see trees outlined by the neon beer-signs, a traffic jam, the source of the music. No people, but cars and trucks were evidence of them. Beyond that, past the Mexican city of Nuevo Laredo, was a black slope – the featureless, night-haunted republics of Latin America. (*OPE* 22)

Then he boards *The Aztec Eagle*, wet and exhausted, looking for his sleeping car which turns out to be an old one that was a part of an American train. The Mexican trains test Theroux's temperament as a traveller. As the trains are mainly used by the locals who do not interact much with strangers, Theroux often feels lonely and uncomfortable. By their rustic appearance and behaviour, Theroux often finds the local passengers irritating. Besides, he has to deal with frequent delays caused by the poor performance of the railway machinery. There are certain individuals though, who are humorous enough to keep the narrative fresh and moving.

When the train pushes on from Veracruz, Theroux reflects on how geography has played a cruel joke on that part of America, which is notorious for earthquakes. One of the consequences of a severe earthquake is a horrendous slum set up by displaced residents outside of Guatemala City. Some of the inhabitants of this slum have lived there for as long as two years and intend to remain there permanently. Though he is a meticulous observer and recorder, at times he is unable to identify fully with the world through which he is passing. At times his narrative lacks empathy by adopting a tone of nonchalance. Another shortcoming of the book is that, throughout the narrative, there are short digressions that talk about various topics such as Latin American place names, nineteenth-century human sacrifice in El Salvador, and the history of Guatemala, Panama Canal etc.

By the time Theroux reaches Buenos Aires, exhausted, he is barely able to keep his wits. Rationality has been kept alive by his reading of Boswell's *The Life of Samuel Johnson* - "I think if I had not had that book to read as I made my way through Colombia, the trip would have been unendurable" (263). One of the distinctions of *OPE* is Theroux's meeting with Jorge Luis Borges in Buenos Aires. Finally, Theroux reaches his destination Patagonia to find himself amidst large empty spaces, adding up to nothing. The emptiness around him does not give him the impression that he has reached his destination. He likes to be on the move, on the train, as Youngs rightly says, "Theroux does indeed delay his arrival until the end of his book . . ." (*Cambridge Introduction* 162).

After the publication of his first two travelogues, Theroux establishes himself as a cognoscente of train travel. Taking the Chinese proverb, "You can always fool a foreigner" as a personal challenge, in 1988, Theroux published *The Iron Rooster,* which records his yearlong excursions in China. He starts his journey anonymously with a group of tourists from London, which is not likely his usual way of travelling. At Mangolina, he separates himself from the group and spends a year criss-crossing China by train. When the government notices the presence of an American citizen roaming around in their country, they assign a humourless Chinese bureaucrat as a chaperone to accompany Theroux. This causes some inconvenience to the solitary traveller.

In China, he visits some of the major business, cultural, and industrial centres, including Beijing, Guangzhou, and Manchuria, and some remote villages. He keeps himself away from the tourist spots and focuses on the little-known destinations accessible by train. Along the way, he converses with hundreds of locals, recording their memories about the Cultural Revolution and the life after Mao Tse-tung. In this book too he makes an effort to impose his generalizations on readers. An example follows:

Everyone [at the train station in Baoji] hawked, everyone spat, sometimes dribbling, sometimes in a trajectory that ran like candlewax down the side of a spittoon. . . . They walked scuffingly, sort of skating, with their arms flapping, with narrow jogging shoulders, or else hustling puppet like, with their limbs jerking. They minced, they plodded, they pushed, keeping their hands out - straight-arming their way -and their heads down. They could look entirely graceless -unexpected in Chinese. (217)

Like in the previous texts, this narrative is also governed by his idiosyncratic condescending tone. The drive to Tibet at the end of the book (no train service then) is memorably rendered and has concluded the book well. The presence of train is pervasive in the text. The book agrees with his own statement, "It is almost axiomatic that the worst trains take you through magical places". (*RIR* 440)

Theroux possesses thorough knowledge about the socio-political background of China, including the hard times of the Cultural Revolution. His expertise thus challenges the Chinese proverb "We can always fool a foreigner". To him, the yearlong journey across a vast nation is a surrealistic experience and he expresses it as: "down I went, bump-bump-bump . . . and down again, bump-bump-bump, until I had fallen halfway around the world" (*RIR* 3).

In *Dark Star Safari: Overland from Cairo to Cape Town* (2002), Paul Theroux travels unaccompanied from Egypt to South Africa to explore the continent he left behind when he had resigned from teaching English as a part of the Peace Corps in Malawi and Uganda decades back. He remembers Africans being proud and diverse, cultures rich in heritage and tradition when the countries were at the brim of independence from European colonialism. He returns to Africa to quench his curiosity to learn what happened when Africa became free. "You'll have a terrible time", one diplomat warns Paul Theroux upon knowing his plans to pull along a desolate road to Nairobi instead of taking an aeroplane. But, "(y)ou'll have some great stuff for your book" (*DSS* 130). Apparently, that seems to be the strategy and motive for Theroux's vanishing into the African continent.

The journey happens in early 2001 and starts in Egypt. Emphasising the colonial slogan "Cape to Cairo railway", the colonial path is substantially followed by Theroux in the course of the book. He tours the ancient Pharaonic sites and also attends an evening at an Egyptian bar at which Naguib Mahfouz, the Nobel laureate, is in conversation with his friends and admirers. As an American, Theroux is environed by questions about the presidents Bill Clinton and George W. Bush as well as the United States' support for Israel. Nonetheless, Theroux realizes then and there that, as an American, he is a natural target for these sorts of responses. Wherever he goes, most of the time, he is approached by the information seekers. Unlike his previous journeys, Theroux cannot take trains the entire way in Africa. But his love for trains is depicted by naming the chapter titles after the train routes.

> I was going to Africa for the best reasons- in a spirit of discovery; and for the pettiest-simply to disappear, to light out. . . . All I had to do was remove myself. . . . I wanted to drop out. . . . The greatest justification for travel was not self-improvement but rather performing a vanishing act, disappearing without a trace. . . . Africa

is the last great places on earth a person can vanish into. (*DSS* 4)

Theroux always exhibits a desire to disappear; he wants to escape from the routines. This induced alienation in terms of space and culture, helps him to be productive. It stimulates his memory, and he writes. He says, "[t]ravel is wonderful it gives access to the past" (*DSS* 64). In the third world, one can have a glimpse of the primeval culture. He mentions about a market in Khartoum which has a medieval setting. By visiting that market, his modern self gets a primordial experience. Later, he says, "African cities recapitulate the sort of street life that has vanished from European cities- a motley liveliness that lends colour and vitality to old folk - tales and much of early English Literature" (*DSS* 186). This exemplifies how effectively Theroux arouses and projects the exotic elements of the place.

> One day, in an African newspaper I read: "In the year 2005, 75 percent of the people in Africa will be living in urban areas." This was only a few years away. *It made me glad I was taking my trip now*, because African cities became more awful—more desperate and dangerous— as they grew larger. They did not become denser, they simply sprawled more, became gigantic villages. In such cities, women still lugged water from standpipes and cooked over wood fires and washed clothes in filthy creeks, and people shat in open latrines. "Citified" in Africa meant bigger and dirtier (*DSS* 268; emphasis added).

Reflecting on a prediction that he comes across, Theroux utters a selfish thought - "it made me glad that I was taking my trip now" (268). In conjunction with the fact that he perceives the news in a cynical way, he delights in his privilege to have arrived early before the villages disappear in Africa. While reading this attitude in the postcolonial context, this glorification of subjective and emotional authorization can be seen as an extension of the imperial exploitation.

In *Ghost Train to the Eastern Star* (2008), Theroux recreates an epic journey that he took thirty years ago, a huge circle by train (mostly) through Eastern Europe, Turkey, the Caucasus, Central Asia, the Indian Subcontinent, China, Japan, and Siberia, crossing all of Asia from top to bottom, and end to end. In the three decades since he first travelled this route, Asia has undergone remarkable changes: "The decision to return to any early scene in your life is dangerous but irresistible," he notes, "not as a search for lost time but for the grotesquerie of what happened since" (*GTES* 3). From the Khmer Rouge torture chambers in Cambodia to brothels in Singapore and bustling call centres in India, Theroux describes the people, cultures, religions, foods, and sex shops that he discovers while lamenting "how gracelessly the world is ageing and all that we have lost" (*GTES* 485).

The narratorial voice is more profound and the humour is not as prominent as in the first text since the text appears more contemplative and denser. This text also contains interesting people such as poor travellers who he shares a train carriage with, a rickshaw driver he gets close with, and a couple of writers too - science fiction legend Arthur C Clarke in Sri Lanka, and Japanese literary scribbler (and marathon runner), Haruki Murakami etc. The text is peppered with political comments and reflections on history. Theroux's ability to describe scenes and people is exceptional but always seems to be followed by a sarcastic note. The reference to his wife as "Penelope" who tells him - "I'm going to do a lot of knitting while you're away" (*GTES* 6) creates the aura of an epic moment in which the hero embarks on a long journey. Perhaps, the invocation of the epic is meant to trace a lineage of his previous grand exploration.

In his second grand journey, geopolitics slightly alters his previous route. He is refused a visa into Iran, avoids Afghanistan because of safety reasons, and so on. Beginning again in London, he takes to the rails through central Europe and Turkey, continuing across various central Asian republics, India, Southeast Asia and Japan. China's "honking" greed for development dissuades him from going there. Then, he flies from Niigata to Vladivostok, and from there rattles back through Russia on the Trans-Siberian Express.

Theroux likes Istanbul, "a city with the soul of a village" (*GTES* 42), and is amazed at the Asiatic glamour of Hanoi, which he visits for the first time. The stories he hears from witnesses of the 1972 Christmas bombing are among the most disturbing in the book. "In Tokyo," he observes, "everyone looks as though they'd all received the same memo: Walk fast and look worried"; whereas the snow-covered emptiness of northern Hokkaido is "the landscape of my dreams" (*GTES* 392). The book concludes with a series of generalizations: "Most people on earth are poor. Most places are blighted and nothing will stop the blight getting worse. Travel gives you glimpses of the past and the future. . . . No one on earth is well governed. . . . The going is still good" (485). The age of the traveller (sixty-seven years) is reflected in his writing as the narrative is more reflective than the previous one. Yet it has clearly failed to make him more tolerant with his experiences in the Third World.

The Imperial Way chronicles an illustrated railway journey through India, from Peshawar, full of Afghan refugees, through Agra, home of the Taj Mahal, to the flooded Chittagong on the Bay of Bengal. About the journey, he says, "neither a vacation nor an ordeal, but rather a kind of sedentary adventuring- an imperial progress along the railways of the old raj" (*IW* 1). He covers Pakistan, India, and Bangladesh, the three countries that now form the political entities which once were a part of British-held India. The mini-narratives are complemented by photographs of the people and places taken by Steve Curry. Though the book is mostly covered by pictures, Theroux paints a real sense of the trains and the people he encounters with his few pages of writing. Along the way, he portrays the countryside and the people who dwell in it, highlighting the fact that the railroads remain as an intrinsic part of the lifestyle of the millions who live in that region. The narrative comprises of colourful accounts of people with extended discussions on the influence of the railways on these people.

At Tungi Junction I saw another train pull in. There were perhaps fifty people clinging to the sides of the engine and hanging from the carriages and sitting and standing on the coach roofs. These seemingly magnetized people had the effect of making the train look small. They completely covered it and of course the paying passengers were jammed inside.

It made me curious about seating arrangements on the Ulka Express. I leaned out of the window and so that, apart from my coach the whole train was exactly the same- people everywhere, holding on to the sides, the engine, and crowding the roofs. (*IW* 29)

The author's enticing description makes the land, and the people come alive, both in squalor and in splendour. The text and photography come in confluence to form a genuinely harmonious account of the everyday lives of people who live around the railways.

Travelling in trains brings the traveller close to the etymological meaning of 'travel', which is 'travail'. By looking at these texts, one can infer that Theroux's retrieval of the mode of rail-travel, is to create an impression of a chivalric deed, emphasising the vulnerability of the travelled body. A solitary journey is often considered heroic, therefore, is valued and esteemed. Loneliness is valorised by Theroux at many instances - "Travel is at its best a solitary enterprise: to see, to examine, to assess, you have to be alone and unencumbered" (*OPE* 182). As he is alone, he invests his time to examine the co-passengers and turn them in to characters of his narratives.

To Theroux, Tim Youngs writes, "fellow passengers and the residents of the places through which he passes are the landscape. The terrain he explores is other people, from whom he is constantly marking his difference" (*Cambridge Introduction* 80). The narrator's peerlessness and his long and tedious peregrination across the nations secure him the status of an adventurer akin to those from colonial time

3

Writing the Rails

Multiple perspectives, alternative truths and realities are inherent in Theroux's texts. Travel should be understood as an experience between head and heart. The head knows what is going on, mainly the discomfort of travelling in trains is not really a necessity to bear, but his heart, the creative and emotional part finds comfort in the feeling of experiencing the unknown.

Travelogues are records of the autobiographical experiences of an individual, yet they are socially pertinent acts. Narrating the other is a challenging task. It is equally challenging for the reader to decipher the polemics of the narrator's gaze and its recordings. As Holland and Huggan assert, "travel writing, however entertaining, is hardly harmless, and . . . behind its apparent innocuousness and its charmingly anecdotal observations lies a series of powerfully distorting myths about other (often, "non-western") cultures" (8). Many critics have pointed out the ideological implications in Theroux's narratives. Travelogue, as a vehicle of cultural prejudice, invites many postcolonial readings.

Boarding trains, both local and international, to reach the destination is Theroux's habitual way of operating, and it forms a discernible pattern. The rails move through a predictable path which serve as the backbone of the narratives. To embellish this narrative spine, Theroux reconstructs everyday details of his trip, based on the notes he kept, with vignettes of people he encountered and sketches of towns he visited. Throughout these descriptive and anecdotal details of his journey, Theroux weaves a far more personal narrative that includes escape stories, disintegrating romance, a family chronicle of immigration to America - creating a series of mini-histories of people who are on the motion. These mini-narratives and short episodes have everything to do with Theroux's relationship to locomotive mobility and the identity of the traveller he shaped for himself. Thus, the railroad world has also supplied "...a new pattern of narrative construction, a model for a serial and sequenced ordering (a "montage") of narrative situations and events" (Ceserani, "The Impact of the Train").

Theroux's narratives which carry a "visual spectacle of mobility" (Fraser and Spalding 180) offer new perspectives to the reading of the text.

The train made its slow circuit of Paris, weaving among the dark buildings and shrieking frseeeeeeeee- fronnnng into the ears of sleeping women. The Gare de Lyons was alive, with that midnight glamour of bright lights and smoking engines, and across the gleaming tracks, the ribbed canvas over one particular train turned it into a caterpillar about to set off and chew a path through France. (*GRB* 18)

This rapid entry into the city of Paris can be contrasted with the tamed-decelerated movement through a Costa Rican countryside.

It is, for the first third of the trip, a mountain railway, the train travelling along a narrow shelf that has been notched into the mountainside. How narrow? Well, at one point a cow had strayed onto the line. To the left was the sheer mountain wall, to the right the drop into the river; the cow was baffled and for almost a mile she lolloped ahead of the engine, which had slowed so as not to kill her. At times she stopped, put her nose against the mountainside, sniffed at the precipice, then started away again, rocking back and forth, stiff-legged, the way cows run. The track was too narrow to give her space to allow us to pass, so she ran ahead rocking, her tail swinging, for almost a mile on this high shelf. (*OPE* 187)

This paradoxical scene, in which the hefty and speeding machine of transport is becoming docile before a plodding cow, offers a unique spectacle to the readers. It documents the confrontation between nature and technology. Another description reads:

The train plunged out of the tunnel and lost its racket in the sunlight and clear air. We teetered on a mountainside, and the subdued chug of the engine - muffled by the tide of air - was like a hushed reverence for the ten fertile miles of the Jiboa Valley, which began at the tunnel entrance and descended as evenly as a ski slope before rising at the foot of the volcano. The volcano was a darker green than the landscape it sprang out of, and it had leonine contours of light and shade, some like shoulders and forepaws, some muscled like flanks and hindquarters. But it had a carved considered look to it and seemed, as I sped towards it on the train,

like a headless sphinx, green and monumental, as if its
head had rolled away leaving its lion's body intact.
(*OPE* 167)

These exhilarating panoramas of the landscapes
impart memorial mobility to the narrator. The visuals and
the perspectives formed are with reference to the
movement in a train's cabin. That is, in such visuals and
perspectives, the train becomes a reference point.
Spalding's comparison between the descriptions of rail
journey and cinematic effects can be used here: "(t)hese
effects- narrative movements, accelerations, and
decelerations- translate into the appearance...[as]
equivalents of the cinema's jump cuts, sweeping
panoramas (or crane shots)" (181). Thus, trains and
railroads not only suggest a background or a theme but also
become a functional and structural part of plot and
narration.

Often Theroux revels in the mechanism of the
railways like in the following passage from *OPE* :

Down the narrowness of the tracks beside the desert the
labouring engine chugged, always seeming on the verge
of spewing its guts out, exploding in a shower of metal
and vapor, or else seizing up in a succession of glugs and
stopping on a slope rolling backwards into the dip, and
going no more. It seemed a marvel that an old engine like
this could keep going, and I came to see the gasps of the
locomotive as energetic rather than feeble. (427)

The working of the old trains often becomes a
description in Theroux's narratives. It marvels him "to see
the gasps of the locomotive as energetic rather than feeble"

(427). In a way, Theroux's attempt is to retrieve the spirit of railways through his texts- "[t]he engine that had taken me to Esquel looked derelict on the siding, as if it would never run again. But it has a hundred more years in it, I was sure" (428).

Railway stations are other focal points in Theroux's texts. Theroux also attempts a cultural reading of the stations and integrates it in his texts. While in the metropolis, the stations are becoming more and more like airports, in remote places like Saigon in Vietnam, locals are not even aware of the location of the stations. Theroux's reference to the stations in Bulgaria and Yugoslavia are interesting by his description of the people there and the food that is offered for sale. Other stations like Bosporus in Istanbul, Howrah station in Calcutta impose landmarks by themselves. Like how Kipling, M. K Gandhi, R.K Narayan and Satyajit Raj, Theroux also identifies the significance of the railways in the Indian society.

India is peculiarly visible from a railway station. I have the idea that much of Indian life is lived within sight of the tracks or the station, and often next to the tracks, or inside the station. It is as if Indians still associate the railway with progress and optimism- certainly in India the railway represents prosperity, and few ambitions could be realised without it. It is not only part of Indian Culture, but it is ingredient in India life: it is dynamic, energetic, powerful. Why else would so many people choose to live so close to it and so easily by sitting at a window seat and watching, one gets a very full idea of Indian society but it is also true to say that Indians keep themselves near the tracks in order to watch the trains go by so that they can see how other people live. (*IW* 15)

Aguiar considers the Indian railway "as an imaginative object" that represents "the culture, forces, and processes around it" (xii), so does Theroux. The passage above exemplifies how Theroux understands the Indian people's intricate association with the railways. It also shows the process of 'transculturation', how India adapts, contests and accommodates the technology to serve their specific needs. Another instance from *IW* delineates how Theroux presents the experience of an unexpected halt on a rail journey in a stereotypical fashion.

> Two hours passed. This is an aspect of train travel that must not be overlooked: the unexplained stop in the middle of nowhere; and the unexplained delay- hours during which only a dog barks, and someone shuts off a radio, and a child emerges from the tall grass beside the track to sell tea in disposable clay cups. You do not know whether you will leave in two minutes or two days so it is dangerous to stray very far from the train. The sun moves higher in the sky. A child begins to weep. Then an unexplained whistle and a few seconds later the train moves, and a five hundred Indians run alongside, trying to board (25)

This detailed and unembellished description offers a realistic portrayal of a railway moment in the Indian context.

Through a brief survey of the railways' presence in literature and a critical reflection on the aesthetic aspects of Theroux's rail narratives, this chapter reveals how railway exists "in a life-world . . . in a vast spectrum of artistic, social and mental practices" (Beaumont and Freeman 9). Literary texts across the world contain rich and diverse images of the railways, reflecting "rational universalism and cultural particularity" (Aguiar 178), modernity and destruction, secularism and class division. "In art, the railway as subject embraced a range of styles from representative realism through impressionism and cubism to surrealism" (Beaumont and Freeman, 9). In travel writing, the mode of transport is efficacious, for it modulates the traveller's experience abroad.

Trains may not be the most modern, the most efficient or even the fastest means of transportation, but trains provide Theroux with the time to be alone, to gather his thoughts and to write in the glow of the landscape he is passing. Theroux frames his encounter with foreign landscapes primarily from train windows:

> ...train travel animated my imagination and usually gave me the solitude to order and write my thoughts: I have travelled easily in two directions, along the level rails while Asia flashed changes at the window, and at the interior rim of a private world of memory and language. I cannot imagine a luckier combination. (*GRB* 188)

Theroux's career as a traveller can be compared to that of a mobile ethnographer. Andre Novoa defines mobile ethnography as follows: "Mobile ethnography is a translation of traditional participant observation onto contexts of mobility. It means that the ethnographer is not only expected to observe what is happening, but also to experience, feel and grasp the textures, smells, comforts and discomforts, pleasures and displeasures of a moving life. It means following people around and engaging with their worldviews." (98) The description of people, their nature, customs, religion, forms of government, and language, is so embedded in travel writing that one supposes ethnography to be indispensable to the genre. A travel writer employs observation and recording techniques of an ethnographer, ultimately creating a text out of thus perceived impressions. Though the modes and techniques followed by Theroux are similar to those used by an ethnographer, the distinction is marked by the haunting presence of the writer's 'home' in the text. It is his superior sense of home that is working behind his analysis of the various cultural forms.

In a globalised world, where facts are known at the tip of your finger, what makes a travel narrative popular is its creation of 'differences'. Travel writing should be understood as a discourse of difference. Debbie Lisle defines travelogues as "[W]ritten by an observing subject about observed objects they are written in the first person from the point of view of the individual making the journey. This results in a firmly established narrator/subject, an active 'I' that uses all of his or her senses to absorb and assimilate the surrounding data and makes sense of it during the act of writing. " (41)

For Theroux, railway is an irresistible element in his life of journeys. Being a story teller, trains are very useful to Theroux. It plays the functional role of getting the characters from one place to another. But there's more to it.

4

The Postcolonial Journeys

Till the mid-twentieth century, travel writing, which was being considered as sub-literary, occupied a marginal place in the hierarchy of genres but was popular among the readers because of the elements of wonder and curiosity. After Edward Said's ground-breaking text, *Orientalism* (1978) that studied non-poetic and non-fictional texts using the methodology that is customarily employed to study the superior genres, there occurred an awakening in the scholarly interest in travel writing. Said connects economic and geographical imperialism to intellectual imperialism which is constituted by cultural forms such as paintings, writings and history texts. He explains the motivations for and the effects of Orientalist discourses, thus showing that literature and culture are not "historically innocent" (*Orientalism* 27). Instead, they carry on "[a] web of racism, cultural stereotypes, political imperialism, [and] dehumanizing ideology" (*Orientalism* 27). Said "shifted the study of colonialism among cultural critics towards its discursive operations, showing the intimate connection between the language and forms of knowledge developed for the study of cultures and the history of colonialism and imperialism" (Young 151). Travel writing, being a form of narrative that had been instrumental in spreading Euro-centric perspectives about the other world, became a significant topic of study in the field of Orientalism. The theory of Orientalism influences many theorists to adopt multidisciplinary approaches to explore the ways in which the West perceive and represent the East in narratives.

Apart from theoretical studies, other disciplines such as History, Anthropology, Ethnography, Geography and Tourist studies find resources in travel writing. Many travel texts were discovered, re-discovered, or re-examined in the process of bringing them back into print and public discourse around this time. Thus, in a world where mobility, travel and multi-cultural encounters become matters of daily life, travel writing gains new relevance and distinction.

The attention to travel writing can be understood as a part of the decanonisation project, which celebrated metanarratives. Smethurst notes that, "the turn to travel writing begins with a non-canonical or even anti-canonical interest in minor literatures, the margins of history, and the work of 'ex-centric' authors, all reflecting a shift towards more pluralistic social and cultural environment since the 1970s" (3). The decades after the Second World War witnessed a gust of commercially successful and profoundly originative travelogues such as Peter Matthiesen's *The Snow Leopard* (1975), Bruce Chatwin's *In Patagonia*, Paul Theroux's *The Great Railway Bazaar* (1975) and *The Old Patagonian Express* (1979), Robyn Davidson's *Tracks* (1980) and so on.

Both railways and travel writing have an intricate association with colonialism. Born in Britain, railways are spread across the world as an efficient tool of colonial expansion. Though it existed in the world since time immemorial, travel writing has played an apparent role in the empire-building. While railways helped in the transportation of people and goods, travelogues gathered and recorded information for the western knowledge system. The duty of imperial travelling subjects was then either to explore and extend the empire, or survey and reconfirm its territories, and the places, and people of the empire. Claire Lindsay notes:

> travel writing not only had volume, popularity and reach during the colonial era, due to its capacity to generate curiosity, excitement and adventure, it was also instrumental in the economy and machinery of Empire: if the imperial centre depended on representations of its peripheries and others to know itself, and to provide a sense of ownership, entitlement and legitimacy, travel writing served up plenty of material for that purpose. (25)

The European explorers worked at the periphery and sent their observations to the centre, mediating between the "world of experience and accumulated knowledge- between the empirical and the imperial" (Smethurst 7). The exploration reports from the far-off colonies disseminated discourses of alterity - "[w]e do it this way, they do it that way may sound neutral but may also contain a "subtext" of superiority and inferiority. And thus, travel writing has been accepted as "one of the ideological apparatuses of empire" (Brown X). A discourse can be understood "as a set of images, vocabularies and material conditions that expresses prevailing truth claims about the world and positions subjects and objects accordingly" (Lisle, *Global* 12).

Since the dawn of the twentieth century, with the "widespread collapse (though not complete erasure) of colonial orders and structures across the world (Lindsay 25)", travelogues also lost their lustre. Around the same time, with the coming of modern motor vehicles and aeroplanes, railways also lost its prevalence in the metropolis and most of the colonies. However, by 1970s, with the arrival of the new-age travellers like Michael Palin, Bill Bryson, Bruce Chatwin and Paul Theroux, the contribution and requirement for travel writings soared high. These writers started presenting their journeys in new style and vigour and succeeded in achieving wide readership across the world. Theroux's rail-narrative is an innovation, which earns him the credit of salvaging a genre. The discursive approach of this chapter starts from the principle that material products both reflect and produce their social contexts; that is, a product like train or its humanist expression – a train journey cannot be understood in isolation from its social, historical and cultural environment.

Paul Theroux, being an American expatriate, who definitely belongs to the privileged group of Western travel writers, is a postcolonial writer. Here, the phrase 'postcolonial' bears a temporal signification, occurring or existing after the end of the colonial rule. Theroux is a well-informed academician who later becomes a crossover writer. His writings bear witness to his deep association with the lineage of Western travel writing. Apart from the typical American affinity for the rails, Theroux's fervour should be critically derived as a characteristic inherited from the colonial times. Exploring the theoretical dimension of his remarkable fascination with the railways suggests that it is his colonial nostalgia that is at work in his rail narratives. The earning for experience and life styles associated with the colonial era is ubiquitous in his texts. This concept which is termed as 'imperial nostalgia', is first proposed by Renato Rosaldo. "Evidently, a mood of nostalgia makes racial domination appear innocent and pure" (68), notes Renato Rosaldo in *Culture and Truth*.

Imperialist nostalgia occurs alongside a peculiar sense of mission, *'the white man's burden,'* where civilized nations stand duty-bound to uplift so-called savage ones. In this ideologically constructed world of ongoing progressive change, putatively static savage societies become a stable reference point for defining (the felicitous progress of) civilized identity. 'We' (who believe in progress) valorize innovation, and then yearn for more stable worlds, whether these reside in our own past, in other cultures, or in the conflation of the two. Such forms of longing thus appear closely related to secular notions of progress. When the so-called civilizing process destabilizes forms of life, the agents of change experience transformations of other cultures as if they were personal losses. (70)

When Theroux scribes that he wants to "make a connection between the known and the unknown" (*OPE* vi), he is echoing the "white man's burden" (Rosaldo 70). It is the feeling of emptiness that stimulates the contemporary writers to go East, in search of "more stable worlds" (Rosaldo 70). When they see changes in the other world too, they lament the loss. Dean MacCannell writes:

For moderns, reality and authenticity are thought to be elsewhere: in other historical periods and other cultures, in purer, simpler lifestyles. In other words, the concern of moderns for 'naturalness,' their nostalgia and their search for authenticity are not merely casual and somewhat decadent, though harmless, attachments to the souvenirs of destroyed cultures and dead epochs. They are also components of the conquering spirit of modernity—the grounds of its unifying consciousness. (24)

Travel becomes a bridge for modern subjects to attain the past. Images of the past are no more available in the metropolis. It has to be sought in the third world, where development happens languidly. Caren Kaplan says, "[w]hen the past is displaced, often to another location, the modern subject must travel to it, as it were. History becomes something to be established and managed through tours, exhibitions, and representational practices in cinema, literature, and other forms of cultural production" (35). The train journeys that Theroux undergoes take him to a time akin to the past.

Colonial nostalgia is seen as a practice of cherishing and invigorating the colonial customs in the contemporary world. It is an eventuality of postcolonial developments in the West, a response to a loss of global position or prestige, and treated as a form of reaction-something that arose in the context of a perceived erosion of old geopolitical hierarchies, spatial borders, social boundaries, and lines of identity. This sense of loss must have generated in Theroux as a by-product of his voracious reading of travel texts. The journeys on trains towards Asia entice him with the notion that the "old world still existed" (*GTES* 143). Travelling through the "old world" in an outmoded transport is an expression of his nostalgia. The train thus becomes a 'time machine' that transports Theroux to the past when travel used to be an extraordinary effort and discovering new places was highly esteemed.

MacCannell studies the social relations between the ever-increasing curious tourists and natives and traces the development of "staged authenticity" (91) which is a separated space from "back regions", where real lives belong to (92). It is to the back regions that a traveller like Theroux intends to go. Theroux's texts are abounding with the desire to escape the ready-made tourist routes and to discover the authenticity of foreignness. And the railways fulfil his wishes as trains penetrate through the back regions, where natives live their natural, uninterrupted lives.

The subject position of the writer creates the distinction between the traveller and the observed. A movement or change in atmosphere is necessary for writing a travelogue. It is the movement that creates the difference needed for narrative. "Narrative is also nourished by change; in this sense journey and narrative imply one another" (60), says Todorov.

Theroux's subject position, the White American Male-writer, is crucial when his narratives are being studied for its colonial implications. In the dialectic of representation of others and selves, the politics of positionality matters. Positionality is the concept that refers to personal values, views, and location in time and space. Gender, race, class, and other aspects of identities signify social and spatial positions. One's position affects the knowledge and perspectives the person has about things, both material and abstract. Positionality influences how one understands the world around him or her and that characterises one's "present attitudes: the projection, or the refusal, of the wish to dominate, the capacity to damn, or the energy to comprehend and engage with other societies, traditions, histories." (Said, *Culture and Imperialism* xxii) A close reading of Theroux's travel texts reveals how they contain renascent forms of imperialism.

Travelogues are texts that attempt to impart shape to an incongruent reality. Through travelogues, travel writers practise "discursive ordering and offer their observations as neutral documentations of a stable, single and ordered reality" (Lisle 12). In order to decipher the prevailing ideology at work in contemporary travel writing, a close reading of the texts is required. Reading the travel texts using multiple theories creates new insights, along with keeping the world and its perceptions unfixed.

5

Conclusion

Travel is a deviant practice. It is not merely a movement from one place to another. It is different from the normal displacement - "breaking with established routines and practices of everyday life and allowing one's senses to engage with a set of stimuli that contrast with the everyday and the mundane" (Urry, *Mobilities* 3). Therefore, traveller's tales are treasured. Writing/Registering Travel is not an uncommon practice in today's world. Even the casual marking "travelling to . . . ." on Facebook can be considered as a mini-travelogue. Such becomes travel and its representation pervasive in a globalised world. Surprisingly, its ubiquity does not adversely affect the wide readership and reception that travel narratives enjoy today. 'To know about other' is a universal human instinct and the travel writers' idiosyncratic engagement with that instinct generates narratives of peregrinations.

Technology, since the time it was developed, received muddled reactions from the literary realm since the nineteenth century. With the introduction of inventions like electric telegram, centralised postal services, the railway, the telephone, the automotive industry and aviation, the society witnessed a revolutionary transformation. Technology also became a popular topic in the contemporary literature. The railroad appears in much of fiction during the early-mid Victorian period because its existence caused significant social change. As the railway lines connected more countries, enabling longer journeys, many writers embarked on long expeditions, thus gaining experience that enriched literature. Eventually, railways evolved to play a distinct cultural role as it acts as a channel that allows energy, goods, people and information to move across the nations, thus becoming a transnational icon.

Train journeys are always intriguing, especially when an episode of railways appears in fiction or in film, it arrests the attention of the readers/viewers and makes them sit at the end of their seat, arousing curiosity in them. Theroux exploits this natural curiosity in readers when he recounts his peregrinations. Railways become more a physical condition of possibility and a metaphorical model for his conception of subjectivity. His journeys on the rail cars provide him with a setting for his reflection on the activity he is indulged in, at the same time, metaphorically, they hold out a structure for his understanding of the internal connections, paths of communications, and networks of information in memory. In his narratives, train is featured as a 'time-object', which "encapsulate[s], resonate[s] with, and evoke[s] earlier times" (Smethurst, "Post-Orientalism" 159), a vehicle that carries him to the otherness and also a cultural commodity with which he gauges cultures.

Usually, a travel narrative talks about a particular destination - the encounters, people, traditions, food - that the traveller chooses to visit. Most of them remain silent about the hitherto journey. More than the destination, Theroux's attention is on the very journey towards it. Penguin Classics edition of *OPE*, published in 2008, comes with a new preface which has the purpose of justifying his position as a distinct traveller. He says, "you want to write a novel but you have no subject, no characters, no landscape. So you take a trip- a couple of months, not very expensive, not too dangerous- and you write it up, making it sound harrowing, dramatizing yourself because you are the hero of this . . . This is not my line of work at all" (v). By denying - "this is not my line of work at all", he calls forth the question, how then does it make a distinction. He continues, "I wanted to make a connection between the known and the unknown and yet remain in the Western Hemisphere" (vi). He thinks his journey has a higher purpose of throwing light on the unknown, which echoes an age-old purpose that resulted in the colonial establishment. He presents himself in a privileged position when he expresses his desire a little later - "I wanted to meet unusual people, and give them life" (VII). Before his text begins and even throughout the text, Theroux attempts to convince the readers of his style. His choice of trains was deliberate for it serves his intention to create a distinct style in travel narration as Ihab Hassan states, "In the train book, he has simply found his form" (164).

One of the reasons for his travelogues to succeed today is that they address the growing fear of the Westerners by showcasing places that are different from their surroundings. With globalisation, every place has become known and familiar to people across the world, making the world less exciting and less diverse (Holland and Huggan 2). Engendering differences in a world that is being homogenised is a task undertaken by contemporary travel writers, including Theroux. With their diverse approaches, they attempt to keep the world "heterogeneous, unfathomable, bewildering" (Holland and Huggan 2). Theroux chooses the offbeat path, the railways, to confront the forms of biological and cultural otherness. It is his choice of the railway as his primary mode of transport that primarily helps him conceive the narratives in the way they are.

Travelling in trains brings the traveller close to the etymological meaning of 'travel', which is 'travail'. By looking at these texts, one has to infer that Theroux's retrieval of the mode of rail-travel, is to create an impression of a chivalric deed, emphasising the vulnerability of the travelled body. A solitary journey is often considered heroic, therefore, is valued and esteemed. Loneliness is valorised by Theroux at many instances - "Travel is at its best a solitary enterprise: to see, to examine, to assess, you have to be alone and unencumbered" (*OPE* 182). As he is alone, he invests his time to examine the co-passengers and turn them in to characters of his narratives.

To Theroux, Tim Youngs writes, "fellow passengers and the residents of the places through which he passes are the landscape. The terrain he explores is other people, from whom he is constantly marking his difference" (*Cambridge Introduction* 80). The narrator's peerlessness and his long and tedious peregrination across the nations secure him the status of an adventurer akin to those from colonial times.

Multiple perspectives, alternative truths and realities are inherent in Theroux's texts. Travel should be understood as an experience between head and heart. The head knows what is going on, mainly the discomfort of travelling in trains is not really a necessity to bear, but his heart, the creative and emotional part finds comfort in the feeling of experiencing the unknown.

The following abbreviations are used in the thesis to refer to the works of Paul Theroux.

DSS- Dark Star Safari

GRB- The Great Railway Bazaar

GTES- Ghost Train to the Eastern Star

IW -The Imperial Way

OPE -The Old Patagonian Express

RIR- Riding Iron Rooster

Bibliography

Primary Sources

Theroux, Paul. *Dark Star Safari*. Penguin Books, 2003.

---. *Ghost Train to the Eastern Star.* Penguin Books, 2009.

---. *The Imperial Way.* Houghton Mifflin Company, 1985.

---. *Riding Iron Rooster.* Hamish Hamilton, 1988.

---. *The Great Railway Bazaar.* Penguin Classics, 2008.

---. *The Old Patagonian Express.* Penguin Classics, 2008.

Secondary Sources

Aguiar, Marian. *Tracking Modernity: India's Railway and the Culture of Mobility.* University of Minnesota Press, 2011.

Ashcroft, Bill. "Travel and Power." *Travel Writing, Form, and Empire*, edited by Julia Kuehn and Paul Smethurst, Routledge. 2008, pp. 229-242.

Barber, Lynn. "Making Waves." *Observer*, 20 February 2000, pp. 41, www.theguardian.com/books/2000/feb/20/travelbooks.lynnbarber

Barthes, Roland. *The Eiffel Tower, and Other Mythologies*. University of California Press, 1997.

Bartkowski, Frances. *Travelers, Immigrants, Inmates: Essays in Estrangement.* University of Minnesota Press, 1995.

Bassnett, Susan. "Travel Writing and Gender." *The Cambridge Companion to Travel Writing,* edited by Peter Hulme and Tim Youngs, Cambridge University Press, 2002, pp. 225-241.

Basu, Ferosa, et al. *New Approaches to Twentieth-century Travel Literature in French: Genre, History, Theory.* Peter Lang, 2006.

Baudrillard, Jean. *The Illusion of the End*. Polity Press, 1994.

Beardsell, Peter. *Europe and Latin America: Returning the Gaze.* Manchester University Press, 2000.

Beaumont, Matthew. "Railway mania: The train Compartment as the scene of a crime", *The Railway and Modernity: Time, Space, and the Machine Ensemble,* edited byMatthew Beaumont, Michael J. Freeman, Peter Lang, 2007. pp. 125-154.

Beaumont, Matthew, and Michael J. Freeman, editors. Introduction. *The Railway and Modernity: Time, Space, and the Machine Ensemble,* Peter Lang, 2007. pp. 13-44.

Behdad, Ali. *Belated Travellers: Orientalism in the Age of Colonial Dissolution*, Duke University Press.1994.

---. "The Politics of Adventure. Theories of Travel, Discourses of Power." *Travel Writing, Form, and Empire*, edited by Julia Kuehn and Paul Smethurst, Routledge, New York. pp. 80–94.

Berger, John. *Ways of Seeing*. Harmondsworth, Penguin, 1972.

Bhabha, Homi K. *The Location of Culture*. Routledge, 2012.

Bird H.S. "Mapping the Geographical Imagination." *Class, Leisure and National Identity in British Children's Literature, 1918–1950."* Palgrave Macmillan, London, 2014. pp. 87-112.

Bissell, David. "Passenger Mobilities: Affective Atmospheres and the Sociality of Public Transport." *Environment and Planning D: Society and Space*, vol. 28, no. 2, Apr. 2010, pp. 270–289, https://journals.sagepub.com/doi/ 10.1068/d3909

Bissell, William Cunningham. "Engaging Colonial Nostalgia." *Cultural Anthropology* 20, no. 2, 2005, pp. 215–248.

Brown, Christopher K. *Encyclopedia of Travel Literature*, Oxford: ABC-Clio, 2000.

Caesar, Terry. *Forgiving the Boundaries: Home as Abroad in American Travel Writing*. University of Georgia Press, 1995.

Cameron, Catherine M., and John B. Gatewood, "The Authentic Interior: Questing Gemeinschaft." *Human Organization*, Vol. 53, No. 1, 1994, www.lehigh.edu/~jbg1/QuestingGemeinschaft.pdf

Carter, Ian. *Railway and Culture in Britain: The Epitome of Modernity*. Manchester University Press, 2001.

Certeau, Michel. *The Practice of Everyday Life*. University of California Press, 1988.

Ceserani, Remo. "The Impact of the Train on Modern Literary Imagination". *Stanford Humanities Review*, Volume 1.1, 1999, web.stanford.edu/group/SHR/71/html/ceserani.html

Chatterji, Arup K. *The Purveyors of Destiny: A Cultural Biography of the Indian Railways*. Bloomsbury Publishing India Pvt. Ltd, 2017.

Clifford, James. *Routes: Travel and Translation in the Late Twentieth Century*. Cambridge: Harvard UP, 1997, *Google Books*, books.google.co.in/books/about/Routes.html?id=EDOVAT808fUC

Connolly, William E.. *Identity/Difference: Democratic Negotiations of Political Paradox*. Cornell University Press, 1991.

Conradson, D., and A. Latham. "The Affective Possibilities of London: Antipodean Transnationals and the Overseas Experience." *Mobilities*, no. 2, 2007, pp. 231.

"Contact zone." *Oxford Reference*, www.oxfordreference.com/view/10.1093/oi/authority.20110803095634533

Cook, Ian, and Philip Crang. "The World On a Plate: Culinary Culture, Displacement and Geographical Knowledges." *Journal of Material Culture*, vol. 1, no. 2, July 1996, pp. 131–153, doi:10.1177/135918359600100201.

Crary, Jonathan. *Techniques of the Observer: On Vision and Modernity in the Nineteenth Century*. MIT Press, 1992.

Cronin, Richard. *Imagining India*. Macmillan, 1989.

Decrop, Alain. "Theorizing tourist behaviour." *The Routledge Handbook of Tourism Marketing*, edited by Scott McCabe, 2014, https://www.book2look.com/embed/9781317936190

Derrida, Jacques, and Anne Dufourmantelle. *Of Hospitality*. Translated by Rachel Bowlby, Stanford University Press, 2000.

Derrida, Jacques. *Of Grammatology*. Translated by Gayatri Chakravorty Spivak, Johns Hopkins University Press, 2016.

Doane, Janice L. and Devon L Hodges. *Nostalgia And Sexual Difference: The Resistance To Contemporary Feminism.* Methuen, New York, 1987.

Douglas, Norman. "Arabia Deserta." *Experiments,* 1925, http://gutenberg.net.au/ebooks03/0300311.txt

Dragojlovic, Ana, et al. "Colonial Re-Collections: Memories, Objects, and Performances." *Bijdragen Tot De Taal-, Land- En Volkenkunde*, vol. 170, no. 4, 2014, pp. 435–441, *JSTOR*, www.jstor.org/stable/43817970

Edwards, Justin D. "Postcolonial Travel Writing and Postcolonial Theory." *The Cambridge Companion to Postcolonial Travel Writing*, edited by Robert Clarke, Cambridge University Press, 2018, pp. 19–32.

Emerson, Ralph Waldo. *The Journals and Miscellaneous Notebooks of Ralph Waldo Emerson*. Volume 10, edited by Merton M Sealts JR., Harvard University Press, 1960.

---."The Young American." emersoncentral.com/texts/nature-addresses-lectures/lectures/the-young-american/

Forsdick, Charles. "Travel and the Body: Corporeality, Speed and Technology." *The Routledge Companion to Travel Writing*, 1st Edition, edited by Carl Thompson, Routledge, 2015, pp. 113-123.

Foucault, Michel. *Discipline and Punish: The Birth of the Prison.* Vintage Books, 1995.

Fujii, James A. "Intimate Alienation: Japanese Urban Rail and the Commodification of Urban Subjects." *differences: A Journal of Feminist Cultural Studies*, vol. 11 no. 2, 1999, pp. 106-133. *Project MUSE*, muse.jhu.edu/article/9599.

Fussell, Paul. *Abroad: British literary traveling between the Wars.* Oxford University Press New York, 1982.

Gandhi, M.K.. *Hind Swaraj and Other Writings*, edited by Anthony J. Parel, Cambridge University Press, 1997.

Goswami, Manu. *Producing India: From Colonial Economy to National Space.* Orient Blackswan, 2004.

"Gaze, Colonial." *International Encyclopedia of the Social Sciences*, 24 Oct. 2019,www.encyclopedia.com/social-sciences/applied-and-social-sciences-magazines/gaze-colonial

Griffiths, Gareth, et al. *Post-colonial Studies: The Key Concepts.*

Psychology Press, 2000.

Harris, Patricia, et al. *The Meaning of Food*. Globe Pequot Press, 2005.

Hassan, Ihab, *Selves at Risk: Patterns of Quest in Contemporary American Letters.* The University of Wisconsis Press, 1990.

Holland, Patrick, and Graham Huggan. *Tourists with Typewriters: Critical Reflections on Contemporary Travel Writing*. The University of Michigan press, 2000.

Huggan, Graham. *The Postcolonial Exotic: Marketing the Margins*. Routledge, 2002.

Hulme, Peter. "In the Wake of Columbus: Frederick Ober's Ambulant Gloss." *Literature & History*, vol. 6, no. 2, Sept. 1997, pp. 18–36, doi: 10.1177/030619739700600203.

Iser,Wolfgang. *The Fictive and the Imaginary: Charting Literary Anthropology*. JHU Press, 1993.

Ivison, Douglas. "Travel Writing at the End of Empire: A Pom Named Bruce and the Mad White Giant." 200-219, *English Studies in Canada*, Vol. 29 No 3-4, 2003, journals.library.ualberta.ca/esc/index.php/ESC/issue/view/20

Jenks, Chris. *Visual Culture*. Routledge, 1995.

John, Elwin Susan. "Sketches of Health in Travel Narratives on India." *International Journal Of Travel Writing*, Sep 2013, No. 2.4, *Coldnoon*, coldnoon.com/wp-content/uploads/2015/09/Elwin_Susan_John_Sep13.pdf

Kaplan E, Ann. *Looking for the Other: Feminism, Film and the Imperial Gaze*. Routledge, Newyork and London, 2012.

Kaplan, Caren. *Questions of Travel: Postmodern Discourses of Displacement*. Duke University Press, 1996.

Keirstead, Christopher M. "Contemporary Postcolonial Journeys on the Trails of Colonial Travelers." *The Cambridge Companion to Postcolonial Travel Writing*, edited by Robert Clarke, Cambridge University Press, Cambridge, 2018, pp. 139–154.

Kennedy, Dane. *The Imperial History Wars: Debating the British Empire.* Bloomsbury Publishing, 2018.

Korte, Barbara. *English Travel Writing: From Pilgrimages to Postcolonial Explorations.* translated by Catherine Matthias, Palgrave, 2000.

Kostova, Ludmilla. "Meals in Foreign Parts: Food in Writing by Nineteenth-Century British Travellers to the Balkans". *Journeys*, 4, 2003, 21-44, doi:10.3167/146526003782487728.

Lawrence, D.H. *Sea and Sardinia.* Cambridge University Press, 1997.

Leavenworth, Maria Lindgren. *The Second Journey: Travelling in Literary Footsteps.* Umea Sweden; 2 edition, 2010.

Leong-Salobir, C. Y. "Spreading the word: using cookbooks and colonial memoirs to examine the foodways of British Colonials in Asia, 1850-1900." *The Routledge History of Food*, edited by C. Helstosky, Taylor and Francis, 2015, pp. 131-155.

Lindsay, Claire. "Travel writing and Postcolonial Studies." *The Routledge Companion to Travel Writing*, edited by Carl Thompson, 2015, pp. 25-34, www.routledgehandbooks.com/doi/10.4324/9780203366127.ch3

Lisle, Debbie. "Gazing at Ground Zero: Tourism, Voyeurism and Spectacle." *Journal for Cultural Research,* Volume 8, Number 1, January 2004, doi: 10.1080/1479758042000797015.

---. *The Global Politics of Contemporary Travel Writing*. Cambridge University Press, 2006.

Lofgren, O. "Motion and Emotion: Learning to Be a Railway Traveller." *MOBILITIES*, no. 3, 2008, pp. 331. *EBSCOhost*, search.ebscohost.com/login.aspx?direct=true&db=edsbl&AN=RN2383 54612&site=eds-live&scope=site

Lorcin, Patricia M. E.. "Imperial Nostalgia; Colonial Nostalgia: Differences of Theory, Similarities of Practice?."*Historical Reflections*, 39(3), December 2013, pp. 97-11, *Research Gate*, doi.org/10.3167/hrrh.2013.390308.

MacCannell, Dean. *The Tourist: A New Theory of the Leisure Class*. University of California Press, 1999.

Maoz, Darya. "The mutual gaze." *Annals of Tourism Research*, Volume 33, Issue 1, 2006, pp.221-239. doi.org/10.1016/j.annals.2005.10.010.

Marshall, Ian. "Steel Wheels on Paper: The Railroad in American Literature." Railroad History, no. 165, 1991, pp. 37–62. *JSTOR*, www.jstor.org/stable/43521515

McKeown, Robert. *Eating Dinner, Writing Culture: The Unique Communicative Power of Food and Travel Journalism*. 2016.Carleton University Ottawa, MA thesis.

McLeod, John. *Beginning Postcolonialism*. Manchester, U.K: Manchester University Press, 2000.

Mee, Catharine. *Interpersonal Encounters in Contemporary Travel Writing : French and Italian Perspectives*. Anthem Press, 2014. *EBSCOhost*, search.ebscohost.com/login.aspx?direct=true&db=nlebk&AN=709392&site=eds-live&scope=site

Mitchell, John William. *The Wheels of Ind*. Thornton Butterworth, 1934.

Moore-Gilbert, BartJ.. *Postcolonial Theory: Contexts, Practices, Politics*. Verso, 2000.

Morris, Jan. "The Allure of Travel Writing." *Smithsonian Magazine*, September 2009,www.smithsonianmag.com/travel/the-allure-of-travel-writing-42681966/

Murphy. Thomas D.. *British Highways And Byways From A Motor Car*, Europaeischer Hochschulverlag GmbH & Co, 2010.

Nietzsche, Friedrich. *Human, All Too Human: A Book for Free Spirits*. Translated by R. J Hollingdale, Cambridge University Press, 1986.

Novoa, Andre. "Mobile ethnography: emergence, techniques and its importance to geography." *Journal of Studies and Research in Human Geography* ,Vol. 9, No. 1, May 2015, pp. 97-107, www.humangeographies.org.ro

Nyman, Jopi, and Pere Gallardo. *Mapping Appetite: Essays on Food, Fiction and Culture*. Cambridge Scholars Publications, 2007.

O'Dell, Thomas. "Commute (ke-myoot´) v." *ETN:HEM:Etnologisk skriftserie.* edited byRobert Willim,2006, pp. 87-95.

Patrick, Holland and Graham Huggan. *Tourists with Typewriters: Critical Reflections on Contemporary Travel Writing.* The university of Michigan press. 2000.

Pau Rubiés, Joan. "Travel Writing and Ethnography." *The Cambridge Companion to Travel Writing*, edited by Peter Hulme and Tim Youngs, Cambridge University Press, Cambridge, 2002, pp. 242–260.

Porter, Dennis. *Haunted Journeys: Desire and Transgression in European Travel Writing.* Princeton University Press, 2014.

Posten, Anne. "Found on the Tracks: European Writing on Train Travel." *Words Without Borders*, November 2015, www.wordswithoutborders.org/ article/found-on-the-tracks-european-writing-on-train-travel-november-2015

Pratt, Mary Louise. *Imperial Eyes*: *Travel Writing and Transculturation.* Routledge, 1992.

Probyn, Elspeth. *Carnal Appetites*: *Food Sex Identities*, Routledge, 2000.

Raban, Jonathan. *For Love and Money: A Writing Life.* Harper Perennial, 1992.

Richter, Amy G. *Home on the Rails: Women, the Railroad, and the Rise of Public Domesticity*. University of North Carolina Press, 2005.

Rosaldo, Renato. *Culture & Truth: The Remaking of Social Analysis.* Beacon Press, 1993.

Ryan, Simon. "Inscribing the Emptiness. Cartography, exploration and the construction of Australia." *De-Scribing Empire: Post-Colonialism and Textuality*, edited byAlan Lawson, Chris Tiffin, Routledge, 2002.

Said, Edward. *Culture and Imperialism.* Random House, 2014.

---. *Orientalism: Western Conceptions of the Orient*. Penguin, 2016.

---. "Representing the Colonized: Anthropology's Interlocutors." *Critical Inquiry*, vol. 15, no. 2, 1989, pp. 205–225. *JSTOR*, www.jstor.org/stable/1343582.

Sandburg, Carl. *The Complete Poems of Carl Sandburg.* Houghton Mifflin Harcourt, 1970.

Schivelbusch, Wolfgang. *The Railway Journey: The Industrialization of Time and Space in the 19th Century.* University of California Press, 1986.

Smethurst Paul. And Kuehn, Julia, editors. Introduction. *Travel Writing, Form, and Empire. The Poetics and Politics of Mobility*, Routledge, 2008.

Smith, Sydney. *The Wit and Wisdom of the Rev. Sydney Smith*. Edited by Evert A. Duyckinck, New York: Redfield, 1856.

Spalding, Steven D and Benjamin Fraser. *Trains, Culture and Mobility*, Lexington Books, 2012.

Spurr, David. *The Rhetoric of Empire: Colonial Discourse in Journalism, Travel Writing, and Imperial Administration*. Duke University Press, 1993.

Stilgoe, John R. *Metropolitan Corridor: Railroads and the American Scene*. Yale University Press, 1983.

Sugnet, Charles. "Vile Bodies, Vile Places: Traveling with Granta." *Transition*, no. 51, 1991, pp. 70–85. *JSTOR*, www.jstor.org/stable/2935079.

Tannock, Stuart. "Nostalgia Critique." *Cultural Studies,* no. 9, no. 3, 1995, pp. 456–57.

Theroux, Paul. *Fresh Air Fiend: Travel Writings,* Houghton Mifflin Harcourt, 2011.

---. "Memory and Creation: Reflections at Fifty." *The Massachusetts Review*, vol. 32, no. 3, 1991, pp. 381–400. *JSTOR*, www.jstor.org/stable/25090272.

---. *The Tao of Travel: Enlightenments from Lives on the Road*. Houghton Mifflin, Harcourt, 2011.

Thompson, Carl. *Travel Writing*. Routledge, 2011.

Thoreau, Henry David. *On Walden Pond.* Coradella Collegiate Bookshelf Editions, epdf.pub/thoreau-walden-civil.html

Todorov, Tzvetan. "The Journey and Its Narratives." *The Morals of History*, translated by Alyson Waters, University of Minnesota Press, 1995.

Urry, John, and Jonas Larsen. *The Tourist Gaze 3.0*. Sage Publications, 2011.

Urry, John. *Mobilities,* Cambridge: Polity, 2007.

Vandertop C. "Travel Literature and the Infrastructural Unconscious." *New Directions in Travel Writing Studies*, edited by Julia Kuehn and Paul Smethurst, Palgrave Macmillan, 2015, pp. 129-144.

Vadillo, Ana Parejo, and John Plunkett. "The Railway Passenger; or, The Training of the Eye." *The Railway and Modernity*, edited by Matthew Beaumont and Michael Freeman, Peter Lang, 2007, pp. 45-68

Van Eeden, Jeanne. "The Colonial Gaze: Imperialism, Myths, and South African Popular Culture." *Design Issues*, vol. 20, no. 2, 2004, pp. 18–33. JSTOR, www.jstor.org/stable/1512077

"Voyeurism." *Merriam-Webster.* https://www.merriam-webster.com/dictionary/ voyeurism

Warde, A., and Martens, L. *Eating out*. Cambridge University Press, 2000.

Warwick, Jack. "Imperial Design and Travel Writing: New France 1603–1636", *Travel Writing, Form, and Empire*, edited by Julia Kuehn and Paul Smethurst, New York: Routledge, 2008, pp.80–94,

Watson, Alex. "The Garden of Forking Paths: Paratexts in Travel Literature." *New Directions in Travel Writing Studies*, edited by Paul Smethurst and Julia Kuehn, Palgrave Macmillan, London, 1997.

Watts, Richard. "Senghor's Prefaces between the Colonial and Postcolonial." *Research in African Literatures,* vol. 33 no. 4, 2002, pp. 76-87, Project MUSE, doi:10.1353/ral.2002.0132.

Wilken Rowan, "Seen from a carriage: A rhythmanalytic Study of Train Travel and Mediation", *Trains, culture, and mobility : riding the rails*, edited by Benjamin Fraser, Steven D Spalding, Lexington Books, 2012.

Wilson, Janelle L.. *Nostalgia: Sanctuary of Meaning.* University of Minnesota Publishing, 2014.

Young, Robert J. C.. *Colonial Desire: Hybridity in Theory, Culture, and Race*. Psychology Press, 1995.

Youngs, Tim. *The Cambridge Introduction to Travel Writing*, Cambridge University Press, 2013.

---. "Punctuating Travel: Paul Theroux and Bruce Chatwin." Literature & History, vol. 6, no. 2, Sept. 1997, pp. 73–88, doi:10.1177/030619739700600206.

Zabel, Darcy A.*The (Underground) Railroad in African-American Literature*. Peter Lang, 2004.

Paul Edward Theroux (born April 10, 1941)